1 Who Are We?

Have You Ever Wondered about…

…the universe?

Imagine that the sun is beside you and is the size of a grapefruit. The earth would then be the size of a grain of sand 35 feet away. The moon would be a tiny speck of sand an inch from the earth. Mercury would be 13 feet from the grapefruit; Venus, 25 feet; Mars, 53 feet. All these planets would be revolving around the grapefruit sized sun.

The sun is, as you know, a star. The next closest star, if it were grapefruit sized, would be 1600 miles away from you. If you were going to make a model like this of our entire galaxy you would need about 10 billion grapefruits. And our universe is made up of billions of such galaxies, all moving away from one another faster than the speed of light.

The universe is very, very big, and we human beings are a very small part of it. It could not be an accident that all this exists! Could it really be true that the Creator of all this cares about us? Have you ever wondered how God could remember, to say nothing about care for, one minute person living on a tiny little planet in a small solar system, in one galaxy in our immense universe?

…the environment?

This creation of God, which is immense, is at the same time fragile. Human beings tend to be a little (or a lot!) selfish and self-centered, adapting and arranging their environment for their own comfort. In the process they have lived in ways that have severely damaged the air, water, land, vegetation and animals that inhabit the earth. Wars between peoples have ruined the land and produced poverty and hunger among its inhabitants. Have you ever wondered about what God thinks about some of the messes people have made in the created world?

OLD TESTAMENT / SESSION 1

...relationships?

And what about the fact that every person is unique? God created men and women, people who have different mental and physical abilities, and people of many colors. Under all the jokes, the fears, and pain lie many questions about how God intends our lives to be together. Have you ever wondered how you fit into God's plan for the human community?

The Word about Creation

We study the Old Testament because it helps us understand these questions and more. As you read the stories in this session, ask yourself why ancient people told these stories of creation.

Read Genesis 1:1-2, 4. The earth began as a dark, formless void. What did God create? Highlight or underline in your Bible God's comment about each created thing.

Read Genesis 2:5-25. This is a second creation story. The earth begins without plants or animals or rain. Why were the animals and birds created? Why was a woman created with Adam? What is different about this creation story? What do you think is important about this story?

An Interview with Dr. Noah Tall

I. Wanda No: Dr. Noah Tall, I'd like to ask you about the importance of the creation stories.

Dr. Noah Tall: Yes, a fascinating subject. One of the things we soon discover about the Bible is that nothing is there by accident. The creation stories set the scene for things to come. God loves all that has been created.

Wanda: I know that God loves everything, but are human beings special?

Dr. T: I believe so. We are creatures and need God in every way. Remember Adam? His name comes from the word for "earth" because he is a part of it. But we are also created in God's image. We speak, think, and have rules about what is right.

Wanda: But what about Genesis 1:26? It says people should have dominion over creation. Doesn't that mean that we are in charge?

Dr. T: Ah, yes! But what most people do not realize is that the dominion that is spoken of means to promote what the Hebrew people called shalom. Shalom means peace, health, and well-being for all people and all creation.

OLD TESTAMENT/SESSION 1

And in this task of dominion, humankind needs all the help they can get.
WANDA: You mean God!
DR. T: And also one another. That is one reason Adam needed a partner, an *ezer* (ay-zer), someone who would help and care just as God helps and cares. Adam needed a friend, someone who could care for him, so God took a rib from his side, a sign of equality, and made an ezer for him, a woman. This is a way for the Bible to tell us that we need one another.
WANDA: That brings me to another question. We are all so different. How can we possibly get along?
DR. T: One of the great points of the first chapter of Genesis is that all creation is good, that it works together and is beautiful. And one of the most important points of the second story is that humans need one another and they need to work together. All people must serve others, no matter what the color of their skin or their different abilities, to carry out all that work of helping creation be as beautiful and peaceful as possible.
WANDA: One more question. . . .Why do you think these stories of creation were written?
DR. T: I think, among other reasons, they were written to help us understand who we are, where we came from, and what God's special purposes are for us.
WANDA: How about all you readers out there? Why do you think the stories of Genesis were written?

"I believe that God has created me together with all creatures."
—LSC

A Little Lower than God

The psalmist sat under the night sky and wondered about the mystery of being made in the image of God. "When I look at your heavens, the work of your fingers, the moon and the stars you have established, what are human beings that you should be mindful of them?"(Psalm 8: 3-4). We are a very small part of our enormous universe, but when we work together to serve all other creatures, great and small, we help create shalom, and God is glorified.

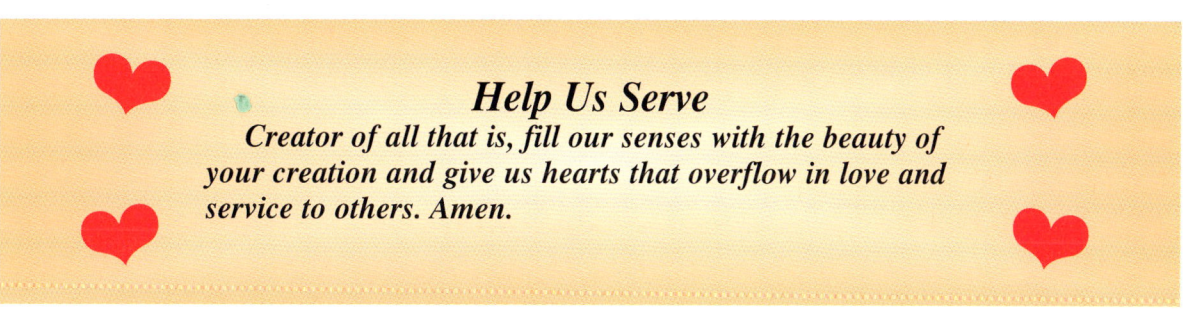

Help Us Serve
Creator of all that is, fill our senses with the beauty of your creation and give us hearts that overflow in love and service to others. Amen.

 Sorry!

Just a Little Lie

Maria had to babysit her little brother, Eddie, on Monday night because her mom worked an extra shift at the hospital. Maria's parents were divorced, her dad lived out of town, and she often had to help her mom.

Babysitting would not be a problem even though she had an important science test. Eddie went to bed at eight and Maria was usually able to get her homework done and still have time for friends and family.

But Monday night turned into a nightmare. Eddie got sick. She tried to read and rock Eddie at the same time, but every time she stopped rocking, he cried. So Maria rocked him until her mom got home at midnight.

The next day, Maria was tired and not ready for her test. She worried all day until her stomach was upset. She was not sure that Mr. Murphy, the science teacher, would think that babysitting a sick brother was an acceptable excuse for not studying. He would probably tell her she should not have left it until the last minute.

Anyway, even though her mom worked extra hard, Maria was embarrassed about her job and did not want to talk about it or her family. She also did not want to fail the test, so she lied to Mr. Murphy and told him that she was sick.

Mr. Murphy was worried about Maria, who really did look sick, and sent her to the office. Even though Maria said she would be all right, the secretary called her mother. Now Maria really felt terrible. Her mother, who had to take time off to take Eddie to the doctor in the morning, had to take more time off to come and pick up Maria at school.

Her mother's supervisor was angry with Maria's mom for taking so much time off from work. Even so, she wanted to take Maria to the doctor. Maria knew that her mom could not afford to take her to the clinic for no reason. Finally, Maria had to tell her mother what happened.

Because of Maria's pride, fear, and procrastination, she was caught by her situation. Maria felt trapped and so she lied to get out of it.

But her lie caused her mother to lose work time and it made her mother's supervisor angry. Maria's mother punished her by grounding her. The secretary and Mr. Murphy found out and no longer trusted Maria.

Maria's actions harmed her relationships with her teacher, the school secretary and her mother. It was just a little lie, but sometimes little lies have big consequences.

It might make you wonder...what exactly is sin? What's the big deal if people sin anyway? What does God do about it?

OLD TESTAMENT / SESSION 2

Sin and Consequences

The Bible, our "library" about God's relationship with humankind, tells us all about sin and its consequences. Through the stories in it we discover that sin:

- existed from the beginning
- tricks us into lying and even violence
- has painful consequences and ruins things
- continues to grow until God intervenes
- is hated by God
- doesn't stop God from caring

A few years ago, the slogan "God don't make no junk" was popular.

The obvious consequences of sins are the immediate painful results such as those Maria and others around her experienced. The longer term results of sin are broken relationships.

Broken Relationships

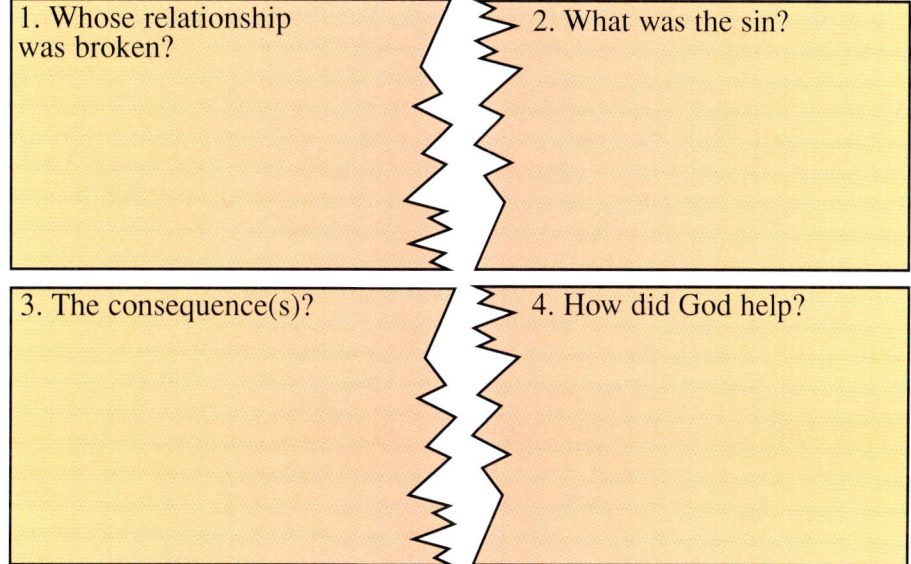

1. Whose relationship was broken?
2. What was the sin?
3. The consequence(s)?
4. How did God help?

A Sorry Mess

When God looked down on creation after sin had a chance to do its dirty work, well, it was a sorry mess. And God said, "I'm sorry I made them." Except for one.

"Noah," God called. "Sorry to tell you this but there's going to be an incredible flood. It will cover everything. So prepare yourself. Build a big ark to save yourself, your family, and the animals."

Noah built it and then the rain came, and everything was destroyed. But God looked at the destruction and was sorry, and decided to never destroy the earth again. The rainbow reminds us of a new beginning with God.

No matter how deep the guilt and how terrible the sin, God still reaches out to us. Just as in Noah's time, God gives us ways to live in spite of our sinful selves. In words like "I'm sorry" relationships are restored with God and one another. The water of Baptism and the bread and wine in Holy Communion are ways to new beginnings in Christ. We still sin, but God reaches out again and again in Jesus.

OLD TESTAMENT / SESSION 2

Dear Earnestine

Dear Earnestine,

My brother and sister fight over the dumbest things. When something bad happens they blame each other. They always do that. What can I do?

Sick of It in Cincinnati

Dear Sick,

I can understand your frustration. Having people pass the buck all the time is tiresome. We all want to be right and perfect all the time, so we would really like to blame others for everything that happens. Instead, we need to own up to our own mistakes. One of the hardest things in life is to take responsibility for our actions. That is something they still have to learn.

Sincerely, Earnestine

Dear Earnie,

I have never gotten along very well with my parents and in the last two years I've done a lot of things to make them mad. Now I want to start over. What should I do?

Regretful in Redwood

Dear Regretful,

Relationships are always a lot of work, but most parents really want to get along. Jesus has given us a way to start over. Try telling your parents that you are sorry for what you have done. You will feel good about yourself and you will be right with God.

Sincerely, Earnestine

Dear E,

I try really hard every day not to do anything wrong. But stuff just seems to happen to me. What do you think?

Dejected in Denver

Dear Dejected,

The apostle Paul, one of the first Christian missionaries, had the exact problem that you do. He said, "I do not understand my own actions. For I do not do what I want but I do the very thing I hate" (Romans 7:15). It's a good thing that God forgives us over and over. And it's good to remember that we are supposed to do the same for everyone around us too! Jesus said we are supposed to forgive others seventy-seven times (Matthew 18:22). Thanks for sharing your story!

Earnestine

Confession

Dear God, life is complicated and sometimes I think I can break the rules. I make mistakes and deliberately hurt others. Sometimes I hurt you. Sometimes I hurt myself. Please forgive me.

Dear (your name here),

I loved the world I created, and I love you so much, that I sent my beloved child Jesus to be your friend, to save you from the harm that sin causes you and others, and to give you a new life. All your sins are forgiven in his name.

"Consequences" Word Jumble

Unscramble the names from Genesis. Choose one letter from each name and fill in the blanks below in order to discover a result of sin.

1. BEAL
2. DOG
3. INCA
4. VEE
5. MADA
6. PRESENT

__ R __ K E __   H __ __ R T __
1   2   3   4   5   6

3 Promises, Promises

Keeping Promises

Take this quick survey on promises. Do you agree or disagree? Number them from 1 to 5 (1=strongly disagree, 5=strongly agree).
___ Most people keep all their promises.
___ Keeping promises is important to me.
___ It's not a big deal whether people keep promises or not.
___ Many people never keep promises.
___ I usually keep my promises.
___ I have trouble trusting people who don't keep promises.

Come on Down

The first 11 chapters of the Bible tell the stories of the beginnings of the world. These stories tell of:
☞ creation and the basic relationships between living things and their creator;
☞ the beginnings of sin and its terrible effects;
☞ how God shows love and mercy in the consequences.

In chapter 12 the story focuses on Abram and Sarai, and the history of Israel. They live in Ur, a city in one of the birthplaces of civilization, in the great valley of the Euphrates River. From there, they travel to Haran to settle in the mountains. But God has plans for them. Read Genesis 12:1-5a.
1. What does God ask Abram and Sarai to do (verse 1)?
2. What does God promise (verses 2-3)?
3. God's call means Abram and Sarai had to move everything and all of their followers with them. Why do you think they moved?

Problems, Predicaments, and Proofs

Once Abram and Sarai have been called, you might think life became easy for them. But this is not what happens. They are supposed to become a great nation, but they have no children. They are led to a wonderful place, but Abram has a troublesome nephew named Lot who takes all the good land and hangs out with the wrong people. They are supposed to bless all the families of the earth, but agreements must be made with local kings who are not happy about a new and powerful neighbor. In fact, their lives are not easy at all. Read Genesis 12:10-20; 16:1-6; 17:15-19; 18:1-14; 22:1-14.
1. In what ways is the promise that God made to Sarai and Abram threatened?
2. The stories of Abram and Sarai demonstrate that being chosen may involve challenges to faith. List the responses of Abram and Sarai to these adventures that confront them.

This map locates the area traveled by Abram and Sarai in relationship to current boundaries of surrounding countries today.

9

Special Delivery

In ancient times, people sometimes changed their names when a significant event altered their lives. Abram and Sarai (whose names mean "exalted one" and "princess") become Abraham and Sarah (whose names now mean "the father and mother of nations") when they are promised a son in their old age (Genesis 17:5,15).

Abraham and Sarah's new names signal a change in their destinies. God keeps the promise of a child, and so the destiny of the whole world is changed as well. When God accuses Sarah of laughing because she doubts she would have a child, she denies it. She is afraid so she says, "I did not laugh (18:5)." When she gives birth to Isaac, whose name means "laughter," she says, "God has brought laughter for me (Genesis 21:6)." Sarah and Abraham's laughter of doubt has become the laughter of joy. Read 21:1-7. Can you think of a time when a promise that was kept by someone you love made you very happy?

Covenants for the Chosen Ones

Over many centuries, God kept the promise to Abraham and Sarah of land, a great nation and blessings to all. The promise God made to Abraham and Sarah is called a covenant. There are other covenants, or promises, in the Old Testament, that God made with people. One was made with Noah, when God promised never to destroy the earth again. Another was made with Moses, when God gives him and the people of Israel the Ten Commandments. These covenants and the tensions that surround them as they seem to be in jeopardy, then fulfilled, are the subject of the entire Old Testament. (*Testament* is yet another name for promise or covenant.)

God called Abraham and Sarah to begin a new people, the Israelites. They responded in faith to God's invitation and they received many blessings. They were chosen to possess the land of Canaan and become a great nation. But more than that they were called to be a blessing to all people.

Those chosen people are our Jewish neighbors, and our ancestors in faith. Christians disagree about our differences with the Jewish people today. But whatever our views, God calls us to love, respect and provide justice for all people. For us Christians, God made a new covenant in our baptisms because of Jesus' life, death and resurrection. We are also called and chosen to belong to God as a new creation and to be a blessing to all people. There is no earthly place attached to the promise, but a heavenly place.

We make many covenants today. Some are stated publicly, and others are simply understood. Men and women make promises when they marry. It is understood that people promise to pay for goods and services. Nations enter into treaties and agree not to harm one another. If no one kept their promises to one another, life would be completely chaotic.

We all can think of times when people break promises to others. People divorce and steal. Nations go to war against old friends. Those instances where trust is breached are painful and harmful. That is what makes our covenant with God special. God is steadfast. God always keeps promises.

OLD TESTAMENT / SESSION 3

A Letter from Our Sponsors

Dearest One,

This morning when we were reading the newspaper, it struck us. We realized that it was 13 years ago today we stood up in front of 200 people and made promises for you. When your mom asked us to be there, we weren't sure we could do it. It's a long trip for us. But we felt honored to make those promises on your behalf, and even though it may sound a little bit grand to you, we felt called by God to do it.

Your baptism was a big occasion, with lots of family and friends all around. You were so small that day, and you have grown so much in every way. We promised to help raise you in the Christian faith, and we promised ourselves that we would be a good example for you, too. In a couple of years, you will make those same promises for yourself, and we will be there when you do it.

What with the way people seem to take their obligations so lightly these days, and break their promises and all, we wanted to let you know that we have always taken that responsibility seriously. We care about you and do our best. But we know it's not easy to follow your call. Sometimes being a Christian is hard, so we pray for you and do our best to help you. But even if we fail somehow, we know that you are God's child, that God has promised to give you a new life, and we know that God will always follow through.

God bless you, dear, and we will see you very soon.

Love,

Aunt Allie & Uncle Rudy

Covenant Keepers

In worship, we who are called to be followers of Christ, gather to express our love for God and for one another. We have been a community of the covenant for centuries. Our seal and sign is the cross that was made on our foreheads when we were baptized. That cross says we are in sacred agreement with God. God keeps that covenant by providing for our needs, forgiving us, and giving us eternal life. We keep the covenant by believing.

Sometimes life is hard and God seems far away. At those times, the community of the covenant helps us, holds us close, prays with us and for us. Sometimes the faithfulness of all believers expresses our faith better than we are able to do ourselves. Thanks be to God for family and friends of the covenant.

4 Cheating, Stealing and Blessing

Genealogical Jazz

You probably take your family for granted. You live in it and it is your everyday reality. But what is it really like?

Families come in all varieties—large and small, emotionally close and distant. Some children's parents live together, others have only one parent at home. In some homes, much of the extended family lives together. Each family is unique and each one is "home" to its members.

In other places around the world families are made up in ways which are different from us. In Saudi Arabia, the law and Muslim beliefs allow men to marry more than one woman. In a few countries, families are discouraged from becoming too large. For example, for many years in China families with more than one child were severely taxed. The opposite is true in many countries where the death rate for infants is very high. Many African families still maintain close tribal ties. Men and women marry only within their extended family, and often an entire city is made up of people who are related. Africans who have lived away from their home towns for many years will often go back to find a suitable husband or wife.

It would be incomprehensible to many of our African brothers and sisters that a family could forget its ancestry. But since most of the people who make their homes in the United States are immigrants, many of them do not know much about their ancestry beyond their grandparents.

In an effort to find out about their past, people have done family histories called genealogies. In them they list all the members of the family as far back as they are able. They often include pictures and little stories of interest about individuals. Alex Haley's book *Roots*, the story of an African American family, is an example of an individual longing to know more about the history of his family. Sometimes, a genealogy is painful. Haley uncovered generations of trickery, slavery, and the agonizing struggle for freedom.

Like *Roots*, a large portion of Genesis is a family history. It is the tale of Abraham and Sarah, the founders of a great nation, their grandson Israel, for whom it was named, and his children. Within this epic narrative are smaller stories filled with trickery, jealousy, romance and the struggle to become a nation.

OLD TESTAMENT/SESSION 4

Gracious God, bless us with your love and help us to bring your blessings to all people everywhere. Amen.

Unlikely Heroes

Throughout the Old Testament, ordinary people safeguard and carry God's blessing to the nations. Abraham and Sarah, while obedient to God's commands, laugh at the notion of having a child in their old age. Isaac and Rebekah play favorites with their children, who come to hate one another. Jacob, who cleverly cheats his brother out of his blessing is in turn cheated by his equally clever uncle. His wives compete with one another, producing a large number of children.

You may feel that none of them deserve God's blessings. God had other ideas. All of these people were faithful in their own way. They believed and carried out God's wishes. They deliberately lived their lives in God's care. The Israelite family history, like the histories of many families, is filled with individual stories of triumph and pain. It is intertwined with the story of God's incredible love, pity, and interactions with each member. That connection gives each life a greater purpose and meaning. It has made all these biblical heroes larger than life.

You may not feel particularly heroic, but you are a part of the great family of God. The Christian family tree has at its base Jesus and all his disciples. Now the blessing is no longer inherited through human parents, or given to the oldest member. Each one on the tree of life has a personal relationship to its founder. Each is a unique member and receives a special blessing from God (read 1 Corinthians 12:12-18). Each branch of the tree is a "hero" in faith and has an important role in the family of God.

It is good to remember that God's heroes are not perfect. They are called and obedient, that is, they deliberately live in relationship with God, depending on God to provide everything they need. God does not set up impossible standards for us to attain, but meets us where we are with plenty of grace.

In a "Dennis the Menace" comic, Margaret says to Dennis, "Mrs. Wilson gives you cookies because she's nice, not because you're nice." Like Abraham and his descendants, we do not deserve God's love. God makes us part of the family, and gives us what we need, out of sheer goodness. God's love for us is a blessing that overflows into every part of our lives.

The Blessing of Blessings

The blessings of our families are important to each one of us. But often, as in the stories of Genesis, favoritism, errors, jealousy and seeming disinterest by our families can hurt us and make us long for more.

God blesses us whether we receive them elsewhere or not. God has:
- created us as unique individuals with special gifts given to us by the Holy Spirit;
- taken an interest in everything about us, in all our happiness and in all our pain;
- invited us to enter into the journey of faith;
- promises to care for us each step of the way
- makes us each into a hero or heroine;
- gives our lives purpose by making us a blessing to others.

14

5
Holding Up under Pressure

Theft of a Good Name

Early one Monday morning, Ricky sat doodling on his notebook and watching Mrs. Morales finish putting math problems on the board. Just as the bell rang, a secretary came in and handed Mrs. Morales a note. She motioned to Ricky.

"Who me?" he asked.

She nodded and told him he was wanted in the principal's office.

When he pushed the heavy glass door open, he saw that Mrs. Gilby, the principal, stood talking to a police officer.

Mrs. Gilby turned to him with a sober face and said, "Ricky, Mr. O'Donnell is here to ask you a few questions about some thefts. He wants to know where you were this weekend."

Ricky's mind spun. Everyone knew that someone had been breaking into cars and stealing radios. He even had his suspicions about who was involved.

"I was just home, just hangin' around."

"Ricky," Mr. O'Donnell said, "some of your friends have said you just bought an expensive bike. Where did you get the money for it?"

Ricky was stunned and embarrassed. He'd saved that money for a long time for that bike. Which of his friends would imply that he'd stolen something? He'd never taken anything. Now someone had stolen his good name.

Have you ever been falsely accused of something? Have you ever been betrayed by someone? Why do you think friends and family members sometimes turn against one another?

FLASH!

Green-Eyed Monster Nabs Colorfully-Coated Boy!

SHECHEM, CANAAN—A boy of seventeen, Joseph, has been killed by a wild animal near Dothan. Apparently, he was sent by his father, Jacob (sometimes called Israel), to check on his brothers and their flocks. He was last seen here, wandering through the fields.

His brothers found his coat covered with blood in a pit near Dothan. His father identified it as one he had made especially for Joseph. The family assumes he is dead. Authorities suspect foul play.

An older brother, Judah, claims that a green-eyed monster devoured his brother. No one has seen it in the vicinity. But his brother Reuben says Judah is known for his sense of humor.

OLD TESTAMENT/SESSION 5

EXCLUSIVE!
The Inside Story

Interview with Jacob and His Eleven Sons

TOM ROLLCALL: Jacob, the bizarre story of your son's disappearance has put you in every major newspaper in the area.

JACOB: Yes, we were all devastated by the news. I just don't understand it! *(At this point Jacob is overcome with tears and leaves.)*

TOM ROLLCALL *(to Jacob's sons)*: What do you think caused Joseph to fall into the pit? Did he have trouble with his vision? And why was he out wandering around by himself?

SIMEON: To be honest, I feel guilty about that. No one really wanted to be with him. We were mean to him. Judah couldn't say a civil word to him.

JUDAH: Oh yeah? What about you?

LEVI: Can we talk off the record? Actually, he was kind of obnoxious sometimes. One time he had a dream that we were all harvesting wheat. We were cutting it down and bundling it together in big bunches called sheaves and our sheaves all bowed down to his. Anybody would get annoyed by that kind of holier-than-thou attitude.

DAN: He was always like that. He had an even more irritating dream. The sun, moon and eleven stars were bowing down to him. He even told our father.

ZEB: And our dad loved it! He gave him great presents like that coat. He always favored Joseph and we finally couldn't stand it anymore.

TOM ROLLCALL: Are you trying to tell me. . . ?

REUBEN: I told them not to kill him!

JUDAH: And we didn't. We didn't want blood on our hands, so we sold him to a caravan.

LEVI: We just put blood all over the coat to fool our father. He still doesn't know.

TOM ROLLCALL: Well, folks. Now you know "The Inside Story."

Stories of the Richly Faithful

Smedley Snerdblad here greeting you from the sumptuous bank of the Nile River. Here at the country residence of Joseph, we can see the result of hard work, forgiveness and, most of all, God's grace.

Not long ago, in a dangerous drought and ferocious famine which he himself predicted, Joseph was reunited with his family from whom he had been estranged for many years. Ignoring the appalling foul play which placed him in constant risk, Joseph forgave his brothers and brought them to live with him in this land of plenty. Friends, this is truly a rags to riches story. And through it all, Joseph's motto has been "God intends it for good."

16

OLD TESTAMENT/SESSION 5

...on Becomes ...ef of Staff

...LIS, EGYPT—A man who has recently ...sed from prison and is known as a dream ...r has become the Pharaoh's new chief of ...

...h's meteoric rise to second in command ...ame about indirectly as a result of his false ...onment. He was a householder for Potiphar ...as imprisoned because of unsubstantiated ...tions made by Potiphar's wife that he ...ed toward her in insulting ways. Others pre-...at the time say that she was angry because he ...refused her sexual advances.

...Undisclosed sources in the local prison identi-... Joseph as a leader and one who had the ...usual spiritual gift of interpreting dreams. ...lace aides acknowledge that Joseph was able to ...terpret an important dream of Pharaoh.

...Though the nation is experiencing bumper ...rops, Joseph says he is planning for a major ...amine which he expects to come in seven years. ...Pharaoh says he "backs him 200 percent."

What Would You Do?

The story of Joseph was told especially for teenagers in Israel as an example of how a faithful man or woman ought to behave when oppressed. No matter how terrible the predicament, God was with Joseph and gave him the courage not only to survive but prosper. Joseph's story is encouragement to those who are trying to hold up under pressure.

- Ali is on the traveling debate team. Every year he tries out for a local play and never gets a role. The director says he is not right for the parts, but you suspect racism.
- The local pizza place recently made the rule that kids under 18 must be accompanied by adults after 8 P.M. Some kids have gotten out of line in the past, but you and your friends have never made any trouble and like to go there after movies.

"You intended to do harm, but God intended it for good...."
(Genesis 50:20)

SERENITY PRAYER

Lord, grant me the serenity
to accept the things I cannot change,
courage to change the things I can, and
wisdom to know the difference.

Let My People Go

Free to...

Place one or more of the following symbols in front of each statement below: a cross if you have heard it in church; a star if you have heard about it in school or in the media; an exclamation mark if you have discussed it with family or friends.

___ No one should be persecuted for their beliefs.

___ Freedom comes with responsibilities.

___ God wants all people to be free.

___ Each person should have the right to vote and determine government policies.

___ We have been freed to serve other people.

___ Freedom is a gift which should be exercised with care so that we do not harm others.

___ God has set us free from sin, death, and the power of evil.

___ We are free to gather to worship.

___ We can hold whatever views we like and speak them publicly.

The Great Drama

Our freedom as Christians has roots as ancient as the Biblical stories. When God's chosen people were enslaved, God set them free.

The book of Genesis ends on a high note. Joseph has been reunited with his family and they have moved to Egypt, into a fertile area called Goshen. They thought that the name of Joseph would protect them forever.

The second book of the Bible, Exodus, takes up the story of God's chosen ones four hundred years later. Time has erased the memory of how Joseph saved the nation of Egypt. Now the Israelites' prosperity has become a fearful problem. Their king becomes their enemy and their neighbors have become their oppressors.

What happened? What characters were important and what was their contribution to the great drama?

Oh, Freedom!

Every day, television, newspapers and magazines bring to our attention the predicaments of people who suffer because they are not free. Some of those people live in countries far away from us. Some live in cities across the country. Some are our neighbors and friends and family members. We live in a world that is far from perfect, where sin has broken many relationships, and many people are oppressed.

Some people, Jewish and Christian, take comfort from the stories of the Passover and the Exodus. In them they recognize many reasons for hope.

When Moses asked God's name, God told him, "I am who I am" which in Hebrew also means "I will be." Believers know that God is always present and actively engaged in

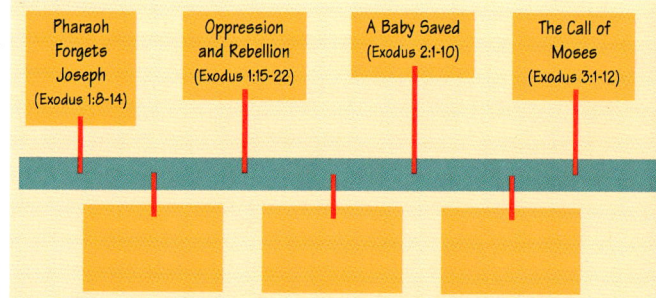

Pharaoh Forgets Joseph (Exodus 1:8-14)

Oppression and Rebellion (Exodus 1:15-22)

A Baby Saved (Exodus 2:1-10)

The Call of Moses (Exodus 3:1-12)

OLD TESTAMENT / SESSION 6

human history on the side of those who are oppressed, and will be in the future as well. They see people called by God and empowered to lead others to freedom.

One of God's leaders for freedom was Harriet Tubman (1820-1913). She lived in the 1800s, when slavery was legal in the United States. At that time more and more people objected to it and especially how it was practiced. Owners were physically and mentally cruel. Marriages between slaves were not recognized, and children were separated from their parents. Slaves were legally denied opportunities for self-improvement. Further, many Christians resented the way slave holders used the Bible to support their beliefs. They said that every sane adult person has a right to freedom, unless they have been convicted of a crime.

Harriet Tubman escaped from Maryland along what was called the Underground Railroad. People who were friendly to those escaping slavery hid them in their houses, fed them and helped them get to Canada. Harriet was nicknamed Moses because she returned to Maryland nineteen times and helped several hundred slaves flee from their bondage.

God has had many other famous allies in the struggle for freedom—Nelson Mandela, who fought apartheid in South Africa; Lech Walesa, who promoted the rights of workers in Poland; Dietrich Bonhoeffer who protested against the Nazi regime and the Holocaust in Germany. Each one resisted the evil of injustice and in doing so put themselves at great risk in order to secure freedom for others.

What are some of the similarities between Harriet Tubman and Moses? between black American slaves and the Israelites in Egypt?

Have you ever suspected that someone was using the Bible to enslave others?

There are many ways to be oppressed. People may endure large-scale oppression, such as what the Israelites and the slaves of early American history experienced. We may also experience racism, sexism, depression, or addiction. God's message to us through Christ is that we have been set free from every oppressor. No one can have our spirit,

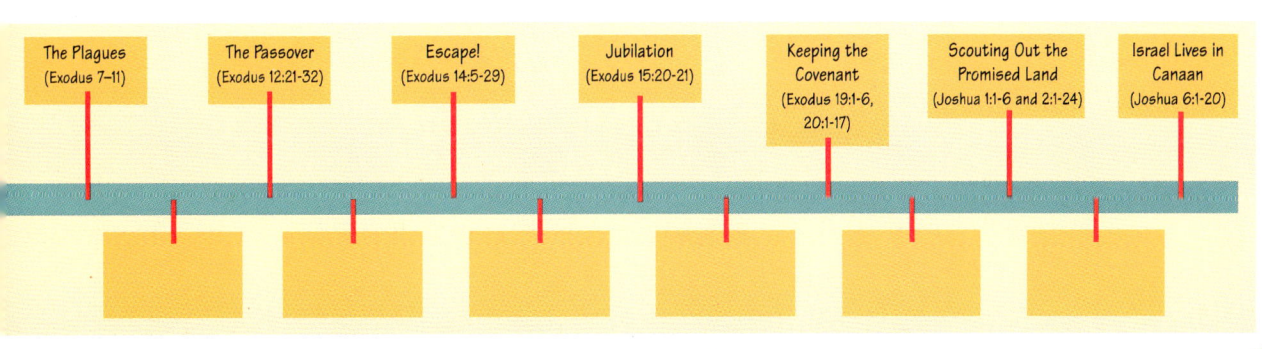

| The Plagues (Exodus 7–11) | The Passover (Exodus 12:21-32) | Escape! (Exodus 14:5-29) | Jubilation (Exodus 15:20-21) | Keeping the Covenant (Exodus 19:1-6, 20:1-17) | Scouting Out the Promised Land (Joshua 1:1-6 and 2:1-24) | Israel Lives in Canaan (Joshua 6:1-20) |

because it belongs to Christ. We are free from sin, death and the power of evil. We are free, not only from human oppressors, but from every kind of enemy. A South African freedom song says it well, "It doesn't matter if they should jail us. We are free and kept alive by hope."

Set Free to Care

Harriet Tubman risked her freedom to set others free. As Christians, we have been freed by Christ from every oppressor. We are free, but we are free to serve.

The reformer Martin Luther said, "A Christian is a perfectly free lord of all, subject to none. A Christian is a perfectly dutiful servant of all, subject to all." We know that God desires justice and freedom for all people. It is easy to become so comfortable about our own freedom and so insistent on our rights that we ignore others. At the same time that we celebrate our freedom, we need to recognize that God's love and freedom belong to our brothers and sisters, too. We remember the needs of others as we celebrate. We are set free, but we are set free to care.

Freedom Psalm

The LORD is my strength and my might,
and he has become my salvation;
this is my God, and I will praise him,
my father's God, and I will exalt him.
Who is like you, O LORD, among the gods?
Who is like you, majestic in holiness,
awesome in splendor, doing wonders?
In your steadfast love you led the people whom
you redeemed; you guided them by your
strength to your holy abode.

Exodus 15:2,11,13

7 Tell It to the Judge

You Be the Judge

For each of the following categories, circle the responses that fit you best. You may choose to circle more than one answer.

1. What do you think about asking for help?
   a. I rarely ask anyone for support or guidance. I prefer to do things on my own. It's embarrassing to ask for help.
   b. I might ask for help if I really trust the person who could help me.
   c. I might ask for help, but only if I was in serious trouble.
   d. I often ask for help. There is nothing embarrassing or wrong about it.

2. I pray...
   a. when I'm in trouble.
   b. all the time.
   c. when something great happens.
   d. in church.
   e. when I'm alone.

3. What do you think about God answering prayer?
   a. God always answers our prayers if we are sincere.
   b. God answers prayers, but sometimes we don't get the answer we want.
   c. I'm not sure if God answers prayers. Anyway, there are times when we should not have what we ask for.
   d. I don't think God answers prayers. I know of times when people have prayed for things that they really needed and they didn't get them.

4. What do you think about God's help in daily life?
   a. People who rely on God for help everyday generally do well.
   b. Some good people have terrible things happen to them, and God seems to have deserted them.
   c. Some people have terrible things happen to them, but still thank God for helping them.
   d. Many people who do things they shouldn't are rich and seem to be happy.

5. My heroes tend to be…
   a. talented pro athletes who are very strong and disciplined.
   b. brilliant scientists who are struggling to understand the world.
   c. great politicians who actively seek justice for everyone.
   d. ordinary people who have accomplished wonderful things.
   e. other_____

6. What do you think about standing against injustice?
   a. People should mind their own business and let other people live their own lives. God helps those who help themselves.
   b. I admire people who fight for others' rights, but I never do it.
   c. I am willing to stand up for my own rights, but have never been involved in struggling for the rights of others.
   d. It is a Christian duty to help people no matter what their circumstances. That includes standing up for everyone's rights.

OLD TESTAMENT/SESSION 7

Help!

The book of Judges is filled with stories about men and women of faith who met God's challenges to promote justice for their people. Each story tells about how the people of Israel had forgotten God and were suffering at the hands of neighboring peoples. When the Israelites asked for God's help, God sent them a judge. Each of these heroes of faith had anxieties or problems. But with God's help, they worked through them and saved their people in spite of their weaknesses.

An example is Deborah, the only Israelite judge who was a woman. She had trouble getting her general, named Barak, to go into battle, presumably because Deborah was a woman. She finally agreed to go with him into battle, and prophesied that the obstinate road he chose to take would lead to an ironic ending. Read Judges 4:1-24.

Put yourself in Deborah's place. Tell exactly what happened that required your services. Who called for God's help? Who called for your help? What were the results? Is there anything that you would do differently if you could? How would you describe God's care of you through all this?

Sometimes God's heroes are almost humorous in the lengths they go to in order to avoid God's call. You will meet the "mighty warrior" Gideon hiding in a wine press, beating the wheat from the chaff. He went into the house and prepared little cakes from more than a bushel of flour, stalling for time. He doubted God and asked for many signs. Finally, he did what God asked him to do.

Read about Gideon in Judges 6:1, 4-6, 11-22, 36-40; and 7:1-22.

Put yourself in Gideon's place. Tell exactly what happened that required your services. Who called for God's help? Who asked for your help? How did you help the people? Why did you hide and ask God for so many signs? What would you do differently if you could do it again? How would you describe God's care of you through all this?

> *"My grace is sufficient for you, for power is made perfect in weakness."*

Patterns of Grace

Have you noticed a pattern in the lives of the people of the Old Testament?
- Abraham and Sarah laughed at the thought of having a child at their old age.
- Isaac was nearly sacrificed by his father and was fooled by his son into giving him a blessing.
- Jacob, Laban and Rebekah manipulated others.
- Jacob's sons threw their brother into a pit and sell him to strangers as a slave.
- Each one of the judges had a personal flaw.

None of God's chosen people were perfect. Instead, they were human and they were faithful. They knew where to look for help.

"I lift up my eyes to the hills—
from where will my help come?
My help comes from the Lord,
who made heaven and earth."

Psalm 121:1-2

OLD TESTAMENT/SESSION 7

Another theme of the Old Testament becomes crystal clear in the stories of the judges. Even when God's chosen people have forgotten who they are, God remembers them and hears them. God uses them and their gifts. God helps them help others.

God's mercy is so wide that every sin and error can be overcome. God's love for us is so deep that it reached all the way to earth in Jesus Christ and saved us on a cross. God's grace still reaches into every corner of our lives, blesses us and shows us how we can overcome every obstacle and help others. When has God called you to be a hero in faith?

Make Us Leaders

Dear God, help us to learn to talk to you every day, to consult with you, to give all our situations to you in prayer. Help us make a difference in the world when we can. Make us leaders in faithfulness by letting you show through our lives. Amen.

Match It

Find the words in the second column that most closely correspond with the numbered words in the first column and write the letter in the space.

___ 1. Judge Deborah
___ 2. Jael and the tent peg
___ 3. Gideon
___ 4. trumpets and smashed pots
___ 5. God
___ 6. Jabin
___ 7. unleavened cakes
___ 8. Sisera
___ 9. fleece
___ 10. Barak
___ 11. the Israelites

a. God's sign to Gideon
b. fed to the angel
c. killed Sisera
d. wouldn't go to war without Deborah
e. King of Canaan
f. they cried for God's help
g. led Barak and 10,000 warriors
h. he had 900 chariots
i. told Gideon he had too many troops
j. was hiding in a wine press
k. confused and scared the enemy

8 Faithful Friends

The Monk's Wisdom

An old story tells about a conversation between a Buddhist monk and handsome king. The young and powerful king asked the old religious man, "Why are you so ugly? You look like a pig to me." The monk merely smiled.

The young king expected the monk to be offended, but he said nothing. The king could not stand the silence, so he asked the monk, "What about me? What do you see when you look at me?" The monk continued to smile and said, "When I look at you, I see Buddha."

The king was amazed. "I told you that you look like a pig, and yet even after I insult you, you tell me I look like Buddha. How can you answer me in that way?" The monk replied, "When you have a pig in your heart, to you everyone looks like a pig. But when you have a Buddha in your heart, everyone looks like a Buddha."

Being a friend, among other things, requires seeing the good in another person. Everyone has faults and the better we know someone, the easier it is to find them and focus on them. It is sometimes much harder to have the heart of Christ, to overlook shortcomings and flaws of character, and see Jesus. What can you do to see the world and all its people with the heart of Christ? Think about it!

Friendship and Redemption for an Outsider

One of the most beautiful stories about friendship is found in the book of Ruth. The book is mainly about three characters who come together in a special way because they were loyal and faithful to one another—Ruth, Naomi and Boaz. Read the book of Ruth and discover extraordinary friendships and redeeming love for a loyal outsider.

What They Said

INTERVIEWER: Tell me about your friends.
ANDREA R: I have different friends for different moods. I have certain friends who I like to be with when I'm in a good mood. But when I'm in other moods, I like to be with others. Like I have some friends I can tell things to that I know will never go out of the room. But some of my friends aren't able to keep a confidence.
SARAH B: They try really hard but they can't do it.
ANDREA R: I have one friend that always tells me that she's not supposed to tell me something and she ends up telling me the whole story.
INTERVIEWER: So confidence is an important thing?
SARAH B: Sometimes. But sometimes I want to be with somebody who can make me laugh. Other times I just want to sit and talk all day. There are some people that can't be serious enough. I have some friends that I can be totally myself with and they don't care. And I have some friends that I have to watch what I'm saying and I have to be a different person. You get nervous even though they're your friend.
A: They make some comments about your hair or something. They're still your friends, and they're still fun, but they have different values.

INTERVIEWER: So would you ever stop a friendship because of how someone looks?
S: Appearances aren't that important to me.
INTERVIEWER: What are your best friends like?
A: My best friends are a girl and a guy. They've been my friends for like years. Best friends aren't exactly like you, but they know what you're talking about right away.
S: I have a best friend and we have the same arguments over and over. But I can't be best friends with a guy anymore because sometimes people take things the wrong way. There's too much pressure from other people.
A: The worst part is being teased. He's not my boyfriend, he's my friend.
S: Society is kind of geared to try and make everything mean something.
INTERVIEWER: Do you have older or younger friends?
S: I was a camp counselor, and some younger friends come over to my house, but I act differently with them. I act more like an adult.
INTERVIEWER: Are you like a mentor to them?
S: It's the same situation with older friends. They are really nice to me. It's good to have that variety. And they've been through it.

I have a mentor for confirmation. She's like my second mom. I trust her a lot. She takes what I say the right way. I look up to her as a person who has been through it and she still has a good sense of humor. I really admire her.

REDEEMER

"One there is, above all others,
Well deserves the name of friend;
His is love beyond a brother's,
Costly, free, and knows no end;
They who once his kindness prove
Find it everlasting love."
(LBW 298)

OLD TESTAMENT/SESSION 8

"I believe that Jesus Christ has redeemed me." —LSC

A: I don't want to worry about what somebody thinks of me. I want somebody who has been through it and will understand me. Some of the older people here are really nice to me.
INTERVIEWER: Do your parents ever try and tell you who you should have as a friend?
A: They say that they trust my judgment. When they don't like someone they tell me that they aren't comfortable with it, but if I am, they'll go along with it.
INTERVIEWER: Have your parents ever been right?
S: Yeah that's the worst part. I think parents look at how someone acts or how they dress, and maybe they're just having a bad day, and they say, "I don't like that person."
A: Sometimes I think parents judge kids too fast. I told my mom that I can't always trust their taste. Her wedding colors were yellow and pistachio, and the groomsmen had ruffles on their shirts.

God as Trusted Friend

Ruth left her native land and provided for Naomi with back-breaking work. Naomi in turn helped Ruth find security by finding a husband for her (unlike today, women in old testament times could not work outside the home and, therefore, depended on a husband to provide for them). Boaz admired Ruth's loyalty, and became *go'el* (redeemer) to Naomi and Ruth. He purchased the land that belonged to Naomi, agreed to marry Ruth, and gave them a new life.

In return, Boaz was blessed with a woman "like Rachel and Leah, who together built up the house of Israel (4:11)." The house of Boaz and the house of Israel were preserved by an elderly widow and her young, foreign daughter-in-law.

The story is more than a story about friendship or how women have preserved the future of Israel. It is an analogy for God's friendship, and how Jesus is go'el and redeemer for each of us.

Like Ruth, God has chosen to befriend us and followed us even into a foreign place in the form of Jesus of Nazareth. Like Naomi, God has brought us home and found us a redeemer, one who can give us new life. And like Boaz, God has taken the responsibility to purchase us. We have been redeemed because Christ died for us.

Like the Buddhist monk, and like a good friend, God looks at us and sees Christ. God is more loyal than our closest friend. God has purchased our lives with the precious blood of Jesus. God is the best friend we will ever have.

9 Glory, Blood, and Corruption

Glory

Every nation has its heroes. Can you tell a story about George Washington? How about Dr. Martin Luther King, Jr? What did Betsy Ross do? Mother Teresa? Nelson Mandela? Cesar Chavez? Yo Yo Ma?

Israel was proud of David and Solomon who were its greatest kings. The kings were not only great warriors, but had other gifts. David was a wonderful musician, and when he played the lyre, he soothed Saul (1 Samuel 16:23). He is credited with writing many of the Psalms (see Psalm 23). Solomon was respected throughout the Middle East for his great wisdom (1 Kings 4:29-30). Even the queen of Sheba came to test him and gave him gold, spices and precious stones. Read how Solomon gained his reputation for wisdom in 1 Kings 3:5-28. During his reign the people were safe and prospered. Read 1 Kings 4:20-25, 32-34.

Blood

One of the most heartrending and brutal stories in the Bible, Rizpah's story, is about a woman with exceptional bravery and compassion (2 Samuel 21:1-14). Her name means "bread baked in ashes." She was a concubine of King Saul and lived in a time of incredible political upheaval, treachery and brutality. Her story tells about the blood on the kings' hands.

Rizpah was widowed when King Saul was killed in battle. (Keep in mind how vulnerable women were who had no husbands.) No one was king yet, and there was a great fight for the throne. At that time, a man named Abner was competing with David for the throne. Abner married Rizpah, which was almost like claiming the throne, because she had been Saul's concubine. Abner was then killed by a friend of David and Rizpah was once again destitute. But the blood bath had only begun.

A drought caused a famine in the land. People in those times believed that God was punishing them for their sins when they went hungry. Today, we look at the climate of the Middle East and realize that it is an arid land. But ancient peoples believed a dry land was cursed by God.

So David tried to discover a reason for the curse. He went to a neighboring people who had a grudge against Saul for breaking a treaty with them. The old treaties were honored because it was the only protection the

WHO IS THE WISEST OF THEM ALL?

1. Who is the wisest person you know? Why?

2. How is being wise different from being smart?

3. What kind of proof would you need that someone is really wise?

OLD TESTAMENT/SESSION 9

OTHER HIGHLIGHTS AND LOWLIGHTS

DAVID'S CAREER
(the highlights):
- a great warrior—"Saul has killed his thousands, and David his ten thousands" (1 Samuel 21:11).
- he consolidated forces and made Israel into a strong nation with its capital in Jerusalem
- he trusted in God

but (the lowlights):
- a disastrous affair with Bathsheba made his own children his enemies (2 Samuel 11,12).

tribes and nations had in ancient times against incessant blood letting. Saul was responsible for the treaties, and was filled with "blood guilt" for trying to destroy his neighbors. The whole sense of community was so strong that even though Saul was dead, his family was still considered responsible for his actions.

When ancient people made a treaty with one another, the parties to it called upon their gods as witnesses and enforcers. They asked the gods to curse whoever broke the treaty. Now David and the Israelites believed that God was enforcing the treaty that Saul broke by causing drought and famine. They asked for the lives of Saul's sons and David agreed. He handed over seven of the sons of Saul, including Rizpah's two sons. They had stakes thrust through them and were left on a mountain to die.

One of the worst things that could be done to a Jewish person was to refuse to bury their remains. There was a curse on those not buried. It was believed that their souls wandered over the earth. So grieving Rizpah took matters into her own hands. She had nothing to lose. She spread her cloak on a rock under the bodies of her children and day and night she chased away the beasts and birds that would have come and devoured them. She sat there for months until the rains came.

When the first rain in three years came, it was evidence that the judgment on Israel for breaking their agreement with their neighbors was over. David was told about Rizpah, sitting vigil for many long days, and he was moved to do the right thing for Saul and his family members. He brought all of their bones and buried them. After all this had been done, after the blood shed and the vigil, and the burial, the rain was plentiful, and the people had food again.

Corruption

Kings were called the shepherds of Israel because God expected them to care for the people like a good shepherd would tend a flock. Initially, it appeared that the kings would do good. But as they became more and more powerful, they were pulled into selfish greed and ambition.

Read Samuel's warning to the people in 1 Samuel 8:10-22. He warned that if they had a king, there would be a tradeoff for national security. He was right. Read about Solomon enslaving his own people in 1 Kings 5:13-17. The king who was brilliant and turned Israel into a showcase became corrupt and no longer cared about God. (Read 1 Kings 11:1-6.)

Eventually, slavery and the breakdown of trust in the king divided Israel in half, much as slavery caused the Civil War in the United States. The north became known as Israel, and the south became known as Judah.

OLD TESTAMENT / SESSION 9

Thy Kingdom Come...

After the kingdom of Israel was divided, it was soon conquered by strong neighboring nations. The people of Israel looked back with longing to a time when they were strong, and prosperous, and when they had shalom. They dreamed of the ideal kingdom that belonged to God.

When Jesus came, he also talked about the kingdom of God, but he was not talking about the same blood, glory, and corruption that had come before. He was talking about a new kind of kingdom and a new king.

The kingdom of God that Jesus referred to over and over is a kingdom where all are cared for and all are free. In this kingdom, the king is selfless, suffering and dying. He builds the world up again at his own expense. In the Lord's Prayer we pray, "Thy kingdom come." We are praying for that new kingdom to come to us.

OTHER HIGHLIGHTS AND LOWLIGHTS

SOLOMON'S CAREER
(the highlights):
- extended the kingdom and amassed great wealth
- built a great temple and fleets of ships
- wrote portions of Ecclesiastes, Proverbs and the Song of Songs

(the lowlights):
- his extravagant tastes led him to bleed his own people dry of resources
- his people came to hate him
- the exploitation of his people led to the greatest disaster in Israel's history - the division of the kingdom

Solve It

Look up the clue and place the circled letter below in the order that you find them. Solve the puzzle to receive a blessing.

1. God promised Solomon a wise and discerning ___ (1 Kings 3:12).   _ _ _ _

2. Samuel warned about the ___ of kings (1 Samuel 8:11).   _ _ _ _

3. The giant David killed   _ _ _ _ _ _ _

4. He had an affair with Bathsheba.   _ _ _ _ _

5. Solomon's people became ____.   _ _ _ _ _ _

6. Solomon and David were _____.   _ _ _ _ _ _

7. Solomon's heart was not true to ___ (1 Kings 11:4).   _ _ _

8. Solomon's court ate 30 ___ of flour every day (1 Kings 4:22)   _ _ _ _

9. He told the people they would cry out because of the king (1 Samuel 8:18).   _ _ _ _ _

_ _ _   _ _ _   _ _ _ _   _ _
_ _ _ _ _ _

Be Our Ruler

God, come to us and reign in our hearts. Make us obedient, loving you and serving one another. Amen.

10 The Voices of God

Looking into the Future

We tend to think of prophets first and foremost as people who can predict future events. Some people believe that by reading the biblical prophecies we can make specific predictions about the end of the world today.

But the biblical prophets did not strictly predict events in that way. They could predict certain short-term events by listening to God and observing the actions of the people around them. One way of

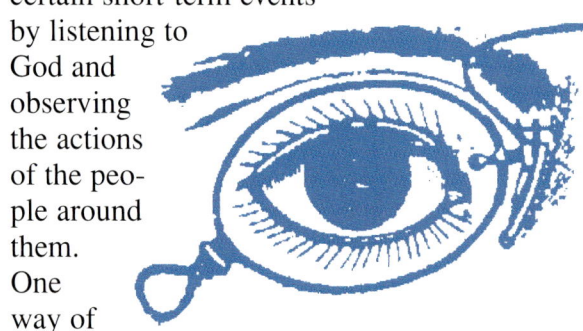

helping understand the predictions of prophets is to imagine exploring a river by boat. You could not map it before you began your journey. You might be able to predict what would happen around the next bend. For example, if the river became more and more shallow and narrow, even though you still had twists and turns ahead you might predict that it would soon end. If you had just travelled down some rapids and heard a loud roar around the corner, you might predict a water fall and stop your journey completely.

The prophets in the Old Testament predicted what they could see and hear next. They warned the people with the information given to them, and they offered hope for a new tomorrow.

IMPRESSIONS NOW AND THEN

Look at the characteristics of prophets and fill in the blank with a *P* if it describes prophets who lived in the past; a *T* if it describes prophets today; and a *B* if both apply.

___ see into the future
___ on late night television
___ dress funny and act strangely
___ advise the king
___ talk about the end of the world
___ stand on street corners yelling at people
___ sometimes are fakes
___ speak God's words to anyone who will listen
___ have a special call from God.

A Passionate God
The Prophet's Call

Each of the prophets in the Old Testament received a special call from God and discovered that God cared deeply about what was happening in their nation. Read about the call of Jeremiah in Jeremiah 1:4-10 and God's first word for the people in Jeremiah 1:14-19.

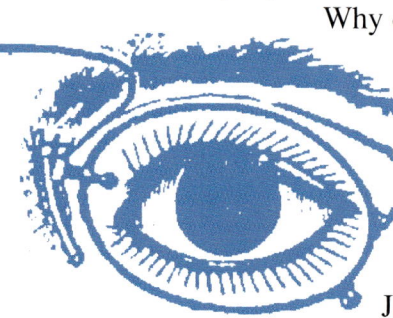

Why did Jeremiah say he was not able to do be a prophet (verse 6-7)? Whose words would Jeremiah be speaking (verse 9)? What effect would they have (verse 10)? Who would carry out God's judgment against Judah (verses 14-15)? God warns Jeremiah that his own people will turn against him (verse 17) and that he must stand up to them. What will God do for Jeremiah (verse 18-19)?

Materialism, Injustice, and Exile

As Israel grew and became prosperous under the kings, the people grew farther and farther away from God. Money ended up in the pockets of a few. Men were violent, and women covered themselves in luxury and were often drunk. They all worshiped other gods, even bringing idols into the temple. But God's greatest heartbreak with the people of Israel was the burden they put on the poor. Read Amos 5:11,15, and 21-24.